PLANT-BA SEAFOOD COOKBOOK

The Complete Cookbook with Easy and Tasty Recipes
for Vegan and Seafood Lovers. Learn How to Eat
and Live in a Healthy and Sustainable Way.
With Colored Quality Pictures!

Lucy Andersen

CONTENTS

INTRODUCTION

Did you know that fish and sea animals feel pain?

Humans, for generations, have fed on sea creatures, creating a storm in ensuring their existence fades away. The flesh of sea creatures can contain high levels of chemical residues and are toxic to humans, hence becoming hazardous to the environment.

Treat these sea creatures and fish like humans: these are complex beings who communicate using squeaks and squeals and other types of body language, have social relationships, and have longer attention spans than humans. Imagine for a second that they did not exist, how would aquatic life be?

To contain the extinction, companies such as Beyond Meat, Upton's Naturals, and Tofurky have introduced plant-based alternatives to seafood animals, quickly expanding their portfolio. You don't have to eat fish when you can enjoy one of the many vegan seafood products that are available online or in grocery stores across the continents in the modern world.

ALTERNATIVE SEAFOOD PRODUCTS

ALTERNATIVE SEAFOOD PRODUCTS

 Sophie's Kitchen

It started in 2011 by introducing a range of fish fillets, shrimps, and canned tuna. Sophie's kitchen bases its products on natural ingredients.
These ingredients include:
- Konjac powder
- Pea starch
- Potato starch
- Sea salt
- Organic agave nectar
- Seaweed powder
- Alginate

As for the products, Sophie's Kitchen produces crab cakes, scallops, smoked salmon tuna, and coconut shrimp.

 Ocean Hugger Foods

Created by Master Chef James Corwell, Ocean Hugger Foods specializes in perfecting the alternative to raw tuna, called Ahimi.
It is healthy and safe to eat an imitation of tuna made from tomatoes. This first product aimed at dishes like sashimi, nigiri, poke, tartare, and ceviche.
In the US, Ahimi is already popular and is sold as a food service ingredient for the B2B food retail market rather than a packaged food product for the end consumer.
Currently, Ocean Hugger Foods are developing additional plant-based seafood alternatives such as Sakimi, which is a carrot-based salmon alternative, and Umami, an alternative based on eggplant.

 Good Catch

This company was founded in 2016 and aims to offer "seafood without sacrifice". Good Catch products contain algal oil, lentils, navy, chickpeas, and fava beans, which resemble the texture of tuna and are a great source of plant-based protein. Their product includes fish-free tuna in different flavors, fish-free burgers, and crab-free cakes.

 New Wave Food

This company develops algae and plant-based shrimp alternatives after being accepted at Indie Bio, the world's largest biotech accelerator.
It also sells its products in the US as a B2B product and is in the process of expanding.

 Nutritional Benefits of Plant-Based Seafood

According to Pilis et al., there is plenty of support for the association that vegetarian diets are a form of a healthy lifestyle in western society: a properly applied vegetarian diet can reduce body mass, improve one's plasma lipid profile, decrease the incidence of high arterial blood pressure, cardiovascular disease, stroke, metabolic syndrome, arteriosclerosis, with the chance for improved insulin sensitivity and lower rates of diabetes and cancer.
Despite some nutrient deficiencies that are possible from a vegetarian diet, "it can be resolved that the beneficial effects of a vegetarian diet significantly outweigh the adverse ones." Considering the surging rates of obesity in the US, vegetarianism is becoming a remedy to many unhealthy tropes related to meat-based fast-food diets.
The benefits of a plant-based seafood substitute diet are unfortunately not widely known. Plant-based seafood offers additional dietary choices where there was none. For people with seafood allergies, these products can be a welcome addition to their diets and offer nutritional benefits as well.
Forbes indicated that plant-based seafood producers boast zero mercury, no fishy smell, no concern of micro-plastics, and a relaxing way to address global overfishing concerns.
Sustainably-sourced seafood can be hard to find and expensive. Plant-based seafood offers an alternative route for seafood lovers who want to do a little less research before digging into a tuna melt or some smoked salmon.
The Food and Agriculture Organization recorded a 122% increase in the amount of fish consumed between 1990 and 2018. In 2017, 17% of animal protein eaten worldwide was seafood, indicating that there is a sizeable place for fish-free alternatives so that fish lovers can still consume the tastes they love, even as seafood continues to increase in demand along with the growing global population of Earth.

GROCERY LIST

GROCERY LIST

You might want to store more vegetarian friendly protein sources if you intend to cut out meat. These are the common vegetarian foods that you will need for plant-based seafood:

Tofu
Seitan
Tempeh
Beans
Eggplant
Chickpea
Cauliflower
Carrots
Tahini
Lime
Coconut milk
Garlic
Coriander
Turmeric
Tomatoes
Legumes
Vegetarian protein powder
Nuts
Lemon

Pantry:
Bread
Canned fruits and vegetables
Quinoa, brown rice, pasta for grains
Jackfruit
Nut butter
Condiments, extract from ketchup and mustard to spicy salsa

Dairy and egg alternatives:

Plant-based egg replacers: often come in liquid and powder form
Plant-based cheese
Nutritional yeast
Flaxseed; used in place of eggs for most vegan baking recipes
Non-dairy milk
Coconut oil or vegetable shortening

Fresh produce:
Fruits
Lettuce, kale, and other greens
Colorful seasonal vegetables
Fresh herbs
Vegetable broth
Chia seeds and sunflower kernels
Crackers, chips, and pretzels
Oatmeal
Oil
Hummus
Dried fruit
Spices and seasonings

RECIPES

VEGAN TUNA SALAD SANDWICH

10 min   20 min   6

INGREDIENTS

- 1 ½ cups chickpeas drained and rinsed
- 1 small stalk chopped celery
- 2 tablespoons dill pickle
- 2 tablespoons vegan mayonnaise
- ¼ teaspoon stoneground mustard
- ¼ teaspoon celery seed
- Pinch dried dill or chopped fresh dill
- Pinch salt
- 8 slices bread

DIRECTIONS

Have yourself an easy-mouthwatering vegan tuna salad sandwich for lunch by swapping out tuna for chickpeas.

Course: Main Course

1. Add the following to a food processor: drained chickpeas, celery, dill pickle, vegan mayonnaise, mustard, celery seed, dried dill, and salt.
2. Beat until flaky and combined, but not to the point of becoming a creamy spread.
3. Spread vegan mayo onto one side of the bread slices. Top four slices with vegan tuna salad, and sandwich them with the remaining pieces of bread.
4. You can add a tablespoon of raw onion to the food processor at this point if you wish.
5. Add dulse flakes to taste if you like fishy flavors.
6. This sandwich tastes good with some pickle slices, onion slices, spinach, and/or tomato as additional toppings.
7. Additional options for vegan tuna salad: put it inside a hollowed tomato, spread it onto crackers, and add it as a topping for a green salad.

NUTRITION

Fat: 19g , Cholesterol: 26.6 mg , Sodium: 824.9 mg , Potassium: 364.9 mg , Carbohydrate: 19.3 g , Calories: 383 Kcal Protein: 32.9 g

CHIPS WITH ALL THE SEASONINGS

5 min   10 min   1

INGREDIENTS

- 1 large Desiree potato, peeled
- ¼ liter vegetable oil

Chili garlic salt, mortar & pestle mix:
- 1 tablespoon fried garlic chips
- ½ teaspoon salt
- ¼ teaspoon sugar
- ¼ teaspoon chili powder

Aussie bush pepper salt, mortar & pestle mix:
- ½ teaspoon salt
- ½ teaspoon Australian native bush peppers
- 1 lemon, zest only
- ¼ teaspoon sugar

Nacho cheese seasoning mix:
- ¾ teaspoon smoked paprika
- ¾ teaspoon onion powder
- ¾ teaspoon garlic powder
- 2 teaspoons nutritional yeast flakes
- 1 teaspoon salt
- ½ teaspoon sugar

Green dressing mix:
- 1 bunch parsley
- 1 bunch dill
- ½ clove garlic
- 1 lemon, zest, and juice
- 1 tablespoon golden syrup
- ¾ teaspoon salt

DIRECTIONS

Deep-fried chips are one of the world's favorite ways to prepare the humble potato. For those preparing this at home, they can get a chance to display their creativity with these mouth-watering seasonings.

1. Prepare your favorite topping
2. Heat vegetable oil to 140°C.
3. Chop potatoes into lengths, to get nice and thick chips.
4. Rinse with cold water.
5. Place the chips in the hot oil for 8 minutes to cook through. Take out of the oil and place it into a tray. Leave for 10 minutes to cool.
6. Raise the temperature of the fryer to 180°C and re-fry the chips for a few minutes until crisped and golden brown.
7. Drain for a few minutes to remove excess oil. Pour into a tray and season with your topping of choice.
8. You can serve with all of your toppings in separate bowls and let people season with their favorite combinations.

NUTRITION

Sodium: 95mg , Calories: 282 Kcal , Fat: 13.4 g Carbohydrates: 33.4 g , Proteins: 4.2 g

VEGAN CRAB CAKES

⏱ 14 min	🍲 6 min	🍽 6

INGREDIENTS

Chickpea artichoke cakes:
- Canola oil or oil spray
- 1 tablespoon vegan mayonnaise
- 14.5 oz can of artichoke hearts
- ½ teaspoon stoneground mustard
- ½ cup chickpeas drained
- ¼ cup chopped red bell pepper
- Zest of one small lemon
- 1 green onion sliced
- ½ teaspoon lemon juice
- ½ cup panko breadcrumbs divided
- 1 teaspoon Old Bay seasoning
- Dash pepper
- ½ teaspoon hot sauce
- 2 tablespoons all-purpose flour
- Pinch salt

Lemon dill aioli:
- 2 tablespoons vegan mayonnaise
- Pinch salt
- ¼ teaspoon lemon juice
- ⅛ teaspoon granulated onion
- ½ teaspoon capers drained
- 1 teaspoon chopped fresh dill – ½ for the aioli and ½ for a garnish

DIRECTIONS

Course: Appetizer

Chickpea artichoke cakes:

Frying the cakes: Fill a non-stick skillet with 1/2 inch of canola oil. Bring to medium-high heat.

Preheat the oven to 400 degrees.

Dry the drained artichoke hearts on a clean kitchen towel, squeeze them to remove any liquid from inside to get them as dry as possible to avoid a wet or sticky cake

Put the drained artichoke hearts, bell pepper, chickpeas, and onions into a food processor.

Beat until they are uniformly broken up. Grate down to ensure everything is evenly incorporated

Put artichoke mixture into a mixing bowl.

Add 1 tablespoon vegan mayonnaise, lemon zest, 1/2 teaspoon lemon juice, Old Bay seasoning, stone ground mustard, 1/4 cup breadcrumbs, hot sauce, all-purpose flour, and a pinch of salt.

Combine all of the ingredients.

Put the 1/4 cup of panko breadcrumbs on a plate.

Add a pinch of salt and a dash of pepper.

Portion out each crab cake using a 1/4 measuring cup.

Coat each side with the panko breadcrumbs on the plate

Ensure the oil is hot enough.

Put a breadcrumb into the oil.

Shallow fry the cakes in the skillet for 3 minutes on one side. Do not overcrowd the cakes in the skillet. Work in batches if necessary.

Once browned on both sides, move them to a towel-lined plate to drain

When baking, put the cakes on a paper-lined baking sheet.

Spritz with oil spray and bake for 20 minutes.

Halfway through, flip the cakes and spray them with oil before returning them to the oven.

Air-frying: Put the cakes into the air fryer tray.

Spritz the cakes with oil spray and air fry at 400 degrees for 10 minutes.

Flip halfway through and spritz the other side with oil

Move the crab cakes to a serving plate.

Top each crab cake with a dollop of lemon dill aioli.

Sprinkle fresh dill for garnish

Lemon dill aioli:

Combine 2 Tablespoons of vegan mayonnaise in a small bowl, granulated onion, 1/4 teaspoon lemon juice, fresh chopped dill, capers, and a pinch of salt.

NUTRITION

Calories: 140 Kcal , Fat: 5 g , Cholesterol: 30 mg , Sodium: 330mg
Carbohydrate: 13g , Protein: 8g

MUSHROOM SHAWARMA WRAPS

⏱ 20 min	🍲 15 min	🍽 4

INGREDIENTS

- 6 large sliced mushrooms
- 3 cloves crushed garlic
- 1 tablespoon maple syrup
- 1 tablespoon of either soy sauce, tamari sauce, or coconut aminos
- ½ lemon, juice, and zest
- 1 teaspoon ground coriander
- 1 teaspoon ground cumin
- 1 teaspoon smoked paprika
- 1 tablespoon olive oil or sub-water
- Salt and pepper

Tahini sauce:
- 2 tablespoons tahini
- ½ lemon, juice, and zest

Serving:
- 8 wholemeal pita bread
- 2 cups shredded lettuce
- 2 medium tomatoes cut into strips
- 1 medium cucumber cut into strips

DIRECTIONS

Mushrooms have an uncanny ability, almost like Tofu, to take on different flavors and seasonings you fancy. This recipe turns mushrooms into the savory 'meat' of a beloved Middle Eastern dish.

1. Toss mushrooms, garlic, lemon, sauce, maple syrup, and spices until combined.
2. Add olive oil or water and mushrooms to a frypan over high heat.
3. Pan fry until mushrooms are soft and cooked through.
4. Add a dash of water to the frying pan to slow down the cooking.
5. Season with salt and pepper to taste.
6. Mix the tahini, lemon, and a dash of water until smooth to make the tahini sauce.
7. Mix in more water for a thinner sauce.
8. Top half the pita slices of bread with mushrooms, tomato, cucumber lettuce, and tahini sauce.
9. Fold over the bread to serve.

NUTRITION

Carbohydrate: 32.22 g , Protein: 8.83 g , Calories: 243.6 g
Fat: 8.80 g

CRAB RANGOON

🕐 10 min   🍲 26 min   🍽 7

INGREDIENTS

- 1 Tablespoon neutral high heat oil
- 5 Gardein crabless cakes
- 1 teaspoon lemon juice
- ½ teaspoon non-dairy milk
- 8 ounces non-dairy cream cheese
- 3 green onions
- 15 mini filo shells
- Pinch salt
- Dipping sauce (sweet & sour or sweet chili sauce)

DIRECTIONS

The vegan crab rangoon appetizers seem fancy for something easy to put together and can be served during parties.
The appetizers are made in mini-filo cups so that they have the desired crunch without having to fold or fry them. Also, instead of crab meat, vegan crab cakes and non-dairy cream cheese are used.
Course: Appetizer

1. Preheat oven to 350 degrees
2. Bring a skillet to medium-high heat with oil.
3. Add frozen crabless cakes to skillet.
4. Brown for 7 minutes and then take them from the skillet and chop into very small pieces.
5. Return them to skillet and continue browning for a few minutes. Once browned, remove from heat, and set aside.
6. Combine non-dairy cream cheese, lemon juice, and non-dairy milk until light and whipped in a medium-sized bowl.
7. Stir 2 Tablespoons of green onions and 1/4 cup of the chopped crabless cakes
8. Line the filo shells across a parchment paper-covered baking sheet.
9. Top the filled shells with remaining crabless cake pieces and a pinch of salt and bake for 10 minutes.
10. Remove from oven and transfer to a serving platter. Then garnish with the remaining green onions and serve with dipping sauce.

NUTRITION

Calories: 146 Kcal , Carbohydrate: 10 g , Protein: 2.0 g , Fat: 10.0 g

VEGAN CEVICHE

🕐 9 min   🍲 1 min   🍽 4

INGREDIENTS

- 14 oz hearts of palm; drained and sliced
- 12 cherry tomatoes; sliced into either halves or quarters
- 1 avocado; cubed
- ¼ cup onion; diced into small pieces
- 2 tablespoons fresh cilantro chopped additional for garnish
- Juice of 1 lime
- Diced fresh or jarred jalapeño peppers
- Pinch cayenne pepper

DIRECTIONS

It can be served with a favorite cocktail and it is vegan & gluten-free. The Vegan ceviche can be a cool and satisfying appetizer, great for weekend gatherings.
Course: Appetizer

1. Combine hearts of palm, avocado, onion, cilantro, tomatoes, and lime juice in one bowl.
2. Add fresh or jarred diced jalapeño pepper.
3. Garnish with additional cilantro and a pinch of cayenne pepper.
4. Serve with tortilla chips or slices of jicama for dipping

NUTRITION

Calories: 173 Kcal , Protein: 28.75 g , Fat: 1.97 g

VEGAN CAVIAR

⏱ 5 min   🍲 10 min   🍽 8

INGREDIENTS

- 1 small beet about the size of an egg
- 1 cup pearl couscous
- 1 ½ cups water
- ¼ teaspoon salt pinch
- 1 Tablespoon virgin olive oil
- ½ teaspoon lemon zest
- ¾ teaspoon lemon juice
- ¾ teaspoon olive brine
- 1 clove garlic either zested or minced

DIRECTIONS

In this vegan caviar, a sliced beet colors pearl couscous. It's flavored with lemon and garlic and served on water crackers with a swish of creamy almond non-dairy cheese.

Course: Appetizer

1. Peel the beet and cut it into roughly half-inch slices.
2. If beet is larger, cut off a strawberry-sized portion. Cut it into several 1/2-inch-thick slices about an inch long.
3. Put peeled beet slices into a medium-sized pot with pearl couscous, water, and a generous pinch of salt.
4. Bring the pot to a boil.
5. Lower the heat to medium or medium-high once it's boiling.
6. Boil the pearl couscous for 10 minutes.
7. Drain the pearl couscous using a fine-mesh sieve. Remove the beet pieces
8. Move the pearl couscous to a medium-sized bowl.
9. Stir in extra virgin olive oil, lemon juice, brine from a jar of olives, lemon zest, and a clove of minced or zested garlic.
10. Cover the bowl & refrigerate until ready to use.
11. Serve on crackers with a swish of spreadable vegan cheese & garnish of fennel fronds, chives, or dill leaves.

NUTRITION

Calories: 246 Kcal , Fat: 2 g , Carbohydrate: 8.0 g , Protein: 10.0 g

---

SESAME SMASHED CUCUMBER, AVOCADO & NORI SALAD

⏱ 20 min   🍲 5 min   🍽 2

INGREDIENTS

- 2 cucumbers (Lebanese)
- ½ teaspoon black sesame seeds
- ½ teaspoon white sesame seeds

Dressing:
- 1 teaspoon sesame oil
- 1 tablespoon soy sauce
- 2 tablespoons malt vinegar
- Salt and pepper

Serving:
- 1 sheet nori
- 1 avocado
- 2 spring onion
- 1 bunch coriander
- ½ cup steamed rice

DIRECTIONS

To release some juices in this salad, break the cucumber, and allow it to take on the beautiful flavors of the dressing.

1. Chop cucumber into irregular shapes, roughly an inch wide.
2. Put into a mortar and pestle and break up a bit.
3. Wrap them in a clean tea towel and hit them with a rolling pin (Alternative).
4. Toast the sesame seeds and add them to smashed cucumber.
5. Add the soy sauce, sesame oil, malt vinegar, salt, and pepper, and mix to combine.
6. Wave the nori sheet over the flame of the stove until soft.
7. Leave for 5 seconds and the sheet will become crisp.
8. Cut avocado in half, remove the skin, and thinly slice it.
9. Cut the spring onion greens on the diagonal and pick a handful of coriander leaves.
10. Add rice to your serving bowl, top with marinated cucumber mix, avocado slices, spring onion, and coriander.
11. Crush the crispy nori sheet.
12. Pour over any remaining dressing from the cucumber.
13. Mix to serve.

NUTRITION

Calories: 140 Kcal , Fat: 6 g , Sodium: 228 mg
Carbohydrate: 24.0 g , Protein: 6.0 g

CRAB DIP

⏱ 5 min	🍲 5 min	🍽 6

INGREDIENTS

- 2 cups raw cashews (soaked)
- 1 large clove garlic
- ¼ cup unsweetened cashew milk
- 2 tablespoons lemon juice
- 2 tablespoons Dijon mustard
- ½ teaspoon Old Bay seasoning
- ½ teaspoon ground sea salt
- ¼ teaspoon ground paprika
- ⅛ teaspoon onion powder
- ¼ ounce can jackfruit packed in water

DIRECTIONS

Course: Appetizer

1. Drain and rinse the cashews.
2. Blend under high power or food processor
3. Add garlic, cashew milk, and lemon juice, Old Bay seasoning, salt, mustard, paprika, and onion powder.
4. Blend for 2 minutes.
5. Grate on the sides frequently until smooth and velvety.
6. Grate the cashew mixture into a medium bowl
7. Drain and rinse the jackfruit.
8. Shred the jackfruit with a food processor.
9. Put it in the bowl with the cashew mixture. Gently fold until fully combined.
10. Serve with crackers, toasted or sliced vegetables

NUTRITION

Calories: 224 Kcal , Fat: 17 g , Carbohydrate: 15.0 g , Protein: 10 g

CHILI MAPLE NUTS

⏱ 5 min	🍲 15 min	🍽 4

INGREDIENTS

- 1 cup walnuts
- 1 cup cashews
- 1 cup pecans
- ⅓ cup maple syrup
- 2 tablespoons brown sugar
- 2 teaspoons salt
- 1 teaspoon chili powder
- ½ teaspoon ground ginger
- ½ teaspoon ground cinnamon
- ½ teaspoon cayenne pepper
- ¼ teaspoon black pepper

DIRECTIONS

These nuts are a spectacular balance for people who like their sweet with a bit of a kick. For a party, these are ideal.

1. Preheat the oven to 180°C
2. Line a baking tray with parchment paper.
3. Place ingredients into a bowl, and mix.
4. Toast for 10 minutes on the lined tray.
5. Stir the nuts, and toast for 10 minutes until glossy.
6. Remove nuts from oven, cool on a separate plate.
7. After cooling, store in an airtight container for 1 week.
8. Add a ½ teaspoon of finely chopped rosemary to get a great twist on this flavor combo!

NUTRITION

Calories: 170 Kcal , Fat: 32 g , Carbohydrate: 3.0 g , Protein: 4.0 g

RAW KOHLRABI RAVIOLI WITH MUSHROOM BROTH

20 min   30 min   2

INGREDIENTS

- 1 kohlrabi
- Black garlic oil
- 6 cloves garlic
- 60ml vegetable oil
- Mushroom broth
- 60g chestnut mushrooms
- 20g dried shiitake
- 1 clove garlic
- ¼ brown onion
- 1 dried red chili
- Soy sauce to taste
- 20g peas

Filling:
- 1 jar nut-based feta
- 1 lemon, juice & zest
- Bunch kohlrabi leaves

Serving:
- Bunch fresh mint

DIRECTIONS

Ever tried cooking with Kohlrabi? This dish is about to make your day. The mandolin slicer will do the trick, turning the hardy, vitamin-C-packed veggies into excellent little ravioli envelopes.

1. Chop the garlic and place it in a pan with oil.
2. Cook until black.
3. Leave to cool then blitz in a food processor with the oil.
4. Chop chestnut mushrooms and half the dried shiitakes, placing in cold water with garlic, onion and dried red chili Water should cover ingredients.
5. Bring to boil. Reduce to a simmer and cook until there is ¼ of the water. Season with soy sauce. Add in the peas.
6. Blanch kohlrabi leaves in boiling water, sock in cold water, and blitz them with nut feta and lemon juice. Alternatively, you can chop them finely and mix them through the feta along with lemon juice.
7. Peel hard skin of the kohlrabi. Slice the kohlrabi wafer-thin.
8. Place a spoonful of nut feta filling in the center and squeeze together to make little ravioli on each round slice of kohlrabi.
9. Place the ravioli in bowls.
10. Strain larger veggies out of your broth. Pour in some broth with the ravioli, including some peas and chestnut mushrooms. Add some black garlic oil and lemon zest. Top with a few fresh mint leaves.
11. Finely chop purple kohlrabi leaf stems, to sprinkle a little pop of color over the dish for a beautiful final touch

NUTRITION

Calories: 147.85 Kcal , Carbohydrate: 11.04 g , Protein: 2.97 g
Fat: 0.98 g

TOMATO LOX & SCHMEAR BAGELS

30 min   5 min   4

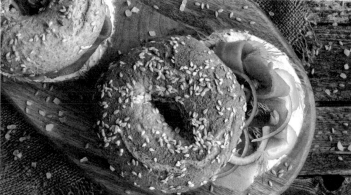

INGREDIENTS

Cream Cheese:
- 400g (14 oz) raw cashews
- 150g (5 ½ oz) dairy-free yogurt (coconut)
- 2 teaspoons lactic acid
- ½ teaspoon citric acid
- 1 teaspoon sea salt
- 2 teaspoons white vinegar
- 1 tablespoon nutritional yeast, plus extra if needed
- 1 lemon juice
- 2 teaspoons capers
- 2 teaspoons of brine
- 1 clove garlic
- A handful of fresh dill

Lox:
- 6 under-ripe tomatoes
- 4 shredded nori sheets
- 125 ml soy sauce
- 1 tablespoon ground ginger
- 1 teaspoon liquid smoke

Serving:
- 4 half-sliced bagels
- 250g (9 oz/ 1 cup) Dill cream cheese
- 1 thinly sliced red onion
- 2 tablespoons rinsed and drained capers
- Dill fronds, to garnish

DIRECTIONS

The smoky and herby flavor combo of a classic 'lox and schmear' bagel with this cashew-based cream cheese and creatively
marinated tomatoes gives a touch and feel of a rich, healthy life!

1. Prepare the cream cheese, soak cashews in cold water for 8 hours.
2. Alternatively, you can boil for 15 minutes, drain, and set aside to cool.
3. Place cashews in a food processor and process for 1 minute, grating down the side of the bowl as necessary.
4. Add yogurt and continue processing until the mixture is smooth.
5. Add lactic acid, salt, vinegar, and nutritional yeast and blitz together.
6. Taste and adjust the flavor if necessary, add more salt or nutritional yeast.
7. Process for a few more seconds until cheese is smooth and creamy.
8. Add zest and juice of 1 lemon, 2 teaspoons of capers along with 2 teaspoons of brine from the jar and add a garlic clove to the cream cheese mixture.
9. Add a handful of dill fronds and beat in the processor until chopped herbs are dispersed.
10. Pop it all in an airtight container in the fridge.
11. Preparing the lox, score a shallow cross into the top of each tomato.
12. Bring a saucepan of water to boil over medium-high heat.
13. Add the tomatoes, and boil for not more than 1 minute.
14. Drain and put the tomatoes into a bowl of cold water to halt the cooking process.
15. Cut each tomato into eight wedges. Pat dry with a paper towel.
16. Place nori in a small bowl of hot water for 1 minute to hydrate.
17. Drain and place in a large bowl with soy sauce, ginger, liquid smoke, and tomato.
18. Set aside in the fridge to marinate for 1 hour or until required.
19. Toast the bagels, smudge 2 tablespoons of dill cream cheese on each bagel.
20. Top with the marinated tomato, red onion, and capers.
21. Garnish with a few dill fronds. Serve warm.

NUTRITION

Calories: 273.91 Kcal , Fat: 2.75 g , Carbohydrate: 55.23 g
Protein: 9.86 g

BROCCOLI, CRANBERRY & CASHEW PIZZA

20 min | 10 min | 2

INGREDIENTS

Pizza dough:
- 1 cup coconut yogurt
- 1 cup self-raising flour and an extra to knead
- 1 teaspoon virgin olive oil
- Salt and pepper
- 1 teaspoon fresh lemon juice

Toppings:
- 2 cloves of finely chopped garlic
- 2 tablespoons of olive oil
- 1 head of cut broccoli (small florets)
- ¼ cup dried cranberries
- ¼ cup toasted cashews
- 2 cups shredded mozzarella or (plant-based) cheddar
- 1 teaspoon dried chili flakes
- Sea salt flakes
- Freshly cracked pepper

Serving:
- 1 lemon, zest, and juice
- 1 bunch of basil
- A drizzle of olive oil

DIRECTIONS

1. Preheat the oven to 250C.
2. Add sifted flour and yogurt, 1 teaspoon olive oil, lemon juice, and a pinch of salt and pepper.
3. Mix until combined to make the dough in a bowl.
4. Knead on a floured bench until dough is soft.
5. Knead the dough on a clean board, lightly dusted with flour until it comes together in a smooth ball.
6. Roll dough out ½ cm thick and place on a tray lined with baking paper.
7. Mix garlic with 2 tablespoons of olive oil and brush onto the base of the pizza.
8. Add cheese to the base to act as the glue for the other toppings; it melts better on the base of the pizza.
9. Top with broccoli florets, cashews, dried cranberries, and more cheese.
10. Sprinkle with chili flakes and season with salt and pepper.
11. Cook pizza in a hot oven for 10 minutes or until the base has browned and crisped.
12. Serve with freshly grated lemon zest and torn basil leaves on top.

NUTRITION

Calories: 288.8 Kcal , Fat: 5.89 g , Carbohydrate: 46.19 g , Protein: 3.98 g

---

SOUTHERN-FRIED JACKFRUIT DRUMSTICKS

1 Hr 45 min | 10 min | 4

INGREDIENTS

- Two 565g cans young rinsed and drained green jackfruit
- 375ml chicken style stock
- 10 drops liquid smoke
- 1 cauliflower
- 2 teaspoons nutritional yeast
- 1 teaspoon onion powder
- 185 ml aquafaba
- Canola oil, for deep-frying

Drumstick spice mix:
- 110g or ¾ cup plain flour, with an extra for dusting
- 1 tablespoon brown sugar
- ½ teaspoon smoked paprika
- ¼ teaspoon garlic powder
- ½ teaspoon sea salt
- ¼ teaspoon ground sage
- ¼ teaspoon dried basil
- ½ teaspoon onion powder
- ½ teaspoon chili powder
- ¼ teaspoon celery salt
- ¼ teaspoon ground allspice
- Pinch dried oregano
- ½ teaspoon kala namak
- 1 teaspoon MSG/torula yeast

DIRECTIONS

This is super fun to make. It involves bringing together a chicken-like drumstick made from putting together jackfruit and cauliflower, smacked, and fried to perfection. Unbelievably delicious!

Separate the hardcore from the jackfruit and squeeze each piece so that seeds pop out and any excess liquid is removed.
Pull the jackfruit pieces to make strings out of them.
Rinse the remaining brine under warm water.
Squeeze the jackfruit dry.
Put the jackfruit in a saucepan.
Add the stock, nutritional yeast, onion powder, and liquid smoke.
Bring the mixture to boil while occasionally stirring for 10 minutes.
Reduce the heat to low.
Cook for 10 minutes until the liquid has evaporated.
Remove and set aside to cool.
Divide the mixture into four portions.
Cut the cauliflower into quarters starting from the base.
Trim the stalks into a round-like bone shape.
Cut off the florets to get a basic chicken drumstick shape.
Make the Southern-fried cauliflower using the florets
Place a large square of plastic wrap on your work surface and spoon half of one portion of the jackfruit mixture.
Lay a cauliflower drumstick on top of the jackfruit mixture.
Add a portion of jackfruit mixture on top.
Take the four corners of plastic wrap and fold over the jackfruit mixture, twisting to enclose the jackfruit around the florets.
Squeeze the jackfruit mixture to let the excess liquid run down the stick.
Mold the jackfruit inside the wrap to evenly cover the cauliflower.
Mush it into the perfect shape.
Repeat for each cauliflower bone stick.
Place the drumsticks on a tray in your freezer for at least 1 hour to firm up.
Combine the spice mix ingredients in a large bowl.
Pour the aquafaba into a separate shallow bowl.
Heat the canola oil in a large heavy-based saucepan over medium-high heat.
Ensure the oil is heated.
Take them out of the freezer and unwrap the plastic wrap.
Drizzle over enough aquafaba to coat while holding a drumstick in one hand.
Place the drumstick into the spice mix and toss extra on top to coat.
Press the drumstick back into shape.
Repeat the coating process and set it aside while you repeat with the remaining drumsticks.
Cook the drumsticks in two batches, turning constantly, for 5 minutes, until golden on all sides.
Drain on paper towels and serve.

NUTRITION

Calories: 164.0 Kcal , Fat: 9.56 g , Carbohydrate: 15.29 g , Protein: 4.20 g

BEER-BATTERED TOFU WITH TARTARE SAUCE

| 2 Hr 15 min | 20 min | 2 |

INGREDIENTS

- 250g tofu
- 2 teaspoons kelp powder
- ½ teaspoon sweet paprika
- 2 teaspoons garlic powder
- 2 teaspoons salt
- 2 tablespoons olive oil
- Rice bran oil
- Grape seed oil

Tartare Sauce:

- 4 tablespoons of egg-free
  mayonnaise
- 5 gherkins
- 5 diced dill pickles
- ½ lemon and juice

Beer Batter:

- 1 ½ cups plain flour
- 375 ml bottle light beer
  (pilsner)

DIRECTIONS

1. Cut tofu twice so you end up with four pieces.
2. Slice into two triangles by cutting each piece diagonally giving you 8 tofu triangles.
3. Put together the kelp powder, garlic powder, paprika, salt, and olive oil in a bowl.
4. Add the tofu pieces and gently mix to coat.
5. Cover and marinate in the fridge for two hours, or overnight if possible.
6. Combine all the tartare sauce ingredients in an airtight container and put them in the fridge until ready to serve.
7. Before cooking, prepare the batter.
8. Put flour in a bowl, pour the beer over and whisk gently until mixed.
9. Heat a heavy-based frying pan or work over medium-high heat.
10. Add rice bran oil to cover the base.
11. Deep the tofu pieces in the batter, covering them lightly.
12. Cook for 5 minutes on each side, until light brown and crispy, being careful of the hot oil when flipping them over.
13. Drain tofu on paper towels.
14. Serve with lemon wedges and your tartare sauce!

NUTRITION

Carbohydrate: 7.38 g , Protein: 37.45 g , Calories: 244.0 Kcal
Fat: 7.42 g

ASIAN STYLE GUAC

| 15 min | 0 min | 4 |

INGREDIENTS

- 3 avocados
- ½ diced shallot
- 3 thinly sliced kaffir lime leaves
- 1 diced red chili with seeds removed
- 1 tablespoon toasted sesame oil
- 3 limes, juiced
- 2 teaspoons coconut aminos
- Salt
- 3 tablespoons extra virgin olive oil

Serving:

- 1 teaspoon black sesame seeds
- ¼ bunch chopped fresh chives
- 1 packet corn chips

DIRECTIONS

1. Put avocados, lime juice, shallot, sesame oil, lime leaves, chili, and the coconut aminos in a bowl.
2. Mash and mix to bring together.
3. Season with salt and extra lime if it needs a little more zing.
4. Loosen with extra virgin olive oil and stir through.
5. Put into a serving bowl and top with black sesame seeds and chives.
6. Serve with corn chips.

NUTRITION

Calories: 454.3 Kcal , Fat: 28.5 g , Carbohydrate: 49.15 g
Protein: 6.6 g

EGGPLANT & TEMPEH 'MEATBALL' SUB

| 20 min | 30 min | 4 |

INGREDIENTS

- 1 diced brown onion
- 3 crushed garlic cloves
- 2 tablespoons olive oil. You can substitute with water
- 1 small cube chopped eggplant
- 300g packet tempeh, of soy or beans
- 1 ½ cup whole-meal flour
- 1 ½ spelled flour or any flour of choice
- ½ cup walnuts
- ½ pecans, or nut
- ½ cup packed parsley
- 2 tablespoons ground flax
- 2 tablespoons chia seeds
- 1 tablespoon oregano
- 1 tablespoon thyme
- 1 tablespoon rosemary
- 2 teaspoons salt, to taste

Serving:
- 2 cups pasta sauce
- 4 rolls whole-meal
- Lettuce leaves
- Vegan cheese

DIRECTIONS

1. Preheat the oven to 180°C.
2. Heat oil in a large frypan over high heat.
3. Pan-fry the onion for 2 minutes until softened.
4. Add garlic, eggplant.
5. Pan Fry until the eggplant is slightly golden.
6. Add ½ cup water and turn down the heat to medium.
7. Cook until the eggplant is tender.
8. Put the cooked eggplant mixture and the rest of the ingredients into a food processor.
9. Beat until combined ensuring it is not processed too much to prevent it from turning into a puree.
10. Scoop heaped tablespoons of the mixture onto a lined baking tray.
11. Shape the mixture into balls with wet hands.
12. Bake meatballs in the oven for 25 minutes, until the outside, is slightly brown. Allow cooling on the baking tray.
13. Add pasta sauce to a large frypan and heat through.
14. Add the meatballs and gently mix until each one is coated.
15. Cut open the rolls and fill with the meatballs, lettuce, and vegan cheese.

NUTRITION

Calories: 105 Kcal , Fat: 7.47 g , Carbohydrate: 6.47 g
Protein: 1.07 g

ZUCCHINI AND CORN FRITTERS

| 20 min | 15 min | 4 |

INGREDIENTS

Preparing fritters:
- 2 large, grated zucchinis
- Corn kernels
- 200g frozen kernels
- 200g quinoa, cooked
- 150g cornflour
- 1 teaspoon paprika, smoked
- 1 teaspoon salt

Preparing whipped tofu cream:
- 150g tofu, silken
- Lemon juice
- Salt
- Extra virgin olive oil

Serving:
- ¼ cup coriander leaves
- Pickled jalapeños
- ¼ cup mint leaves
- Extra virgin olive oil

DIRECTIONS

Crispy zucchini fritters for brunch are quick and easy to make. They are bound so well by the cornflour so that they are difficult to screw up. Whipped tofu cream is added to make a light tangy yogurt as a sauce.

1. Prepare fritter mix in a bowl.
2. Add the zucchini, cornflour, smoked paprika, corn, quinoa, and salt.
3. Mix thoroughly until you have a chunky batter.
4. Preheat a non-stick frying pan over medium-high heat and allow it to come to temperature.
5. Add olive oil and place heaped tablespoons of the batter into the pan.
6. Spread the batter out if needed so they're roughly even thickness.
7. Cook the fritters for 4 minutes on each side; until golden brown and crispy.
8. Place the silken tofu into the blender with a squeeze of lemon juice, a dash of extra virgin olive oil, and a pinch of salt for the whipped tofu cream to form.
9. Pound on high for a minute until you get a smooth consistency.
10. Adjust the seasoning and set aside.
11. Divide the fritters among 4 plates alongside generous dollops of whipped tofu cream.
12. Sprinkle on your herbs and pickled jalapeños.

NUTRITION

Calories: 96.8 Kcal , Fat: 0.82 g , Sodium: 112 mg
Carbohydrate: 20.37 g , Proteins: 2.79 g

INDIAN CHICKPEA FRITTERS WITH COCONUT CHUTNEY

| 25 min | 20 min | 4 |

INGREDIENTS

Green coconut:
- 1 bunch picked, washed, and chopped coriander leaves.
- ⅔ cup yogurt (coconut)
- 1 clove minced garlic
- 1 hot finely diced green chili
- 2 teaspoons lemon juice
- 1 tablespoon toasted shredded coconut

Fritters:
- 1 ½ cups besan flour
- 1 ½ chickpea flour
- 1 teaspoon cumin
- 1 teaspoon garam masala
- ½ teaspoon salt
- 1 cup water
- 1 small grated sweet potato
- ½ thinly sliced red onion
- ½ cup slightly smashed cooked chickpeas
- 1 cup roughly chopped coriander leaves
- 1 clove finely minced garlic
- 1 small finely diced red chili
- Peanut or vegetable oil

DIRECTIONS

1. Place the coriander, yogurt, garlic, chili, and lemon juice in a bowl. Mix. Keep chilled.
2. Top with toasted shredded coconut.
3. Combine the garam masala, besan flour, cumin, and salt, mix.
4. Add the water and stir to combine for the Fritters.
5. Add ingredients and leave for 10 minutes to thicken slightly.
6. Pour the oil into a large heavy-based pan, about 1 cm deep, and heat.
7. Measure out a large tablespoon of the batter.
8. Carefully lower it into the hot oil.
9. Add one more spoonful to the pan, taking care not to overcrowd.
10. Shallow fry for 5-6 minutes, until crispy and golden brown.
11. Remove with a spoon and place onto a cooling rack.
12. Season well with salt.
13. Continue until all the batter is used up.
14. Serve while hot with the green coconut chutney

NUTRITION

Calories: 246.3 Kcal , Fat: 4.5 g , Sodium: 246 mg
Carbohydrate: 40.5 , Protein: 13.5 g

LENTIL & WALNUT TACOS

| 15 min | 15 min | 4 |

INGREDIENTS

- 500 g button mushrooms
- ½ cup walnuts
- 2 tablespoons olive oil
- ½ onion, finely diced
- 1 garlic clove, crushed
- 1 teaspoon chili flakes
- 1-2 x 28 g sachets taco seasoning, or use seasoning recipe from this dish
- 400 g tin lentils, rinsed and drained
- 8 taco shells

Taco Toppings:
- 1-2 smashed avocados, or this guacamole
- 1 cup cashew sour cream
- 3 cups finely shredded iceberg lettuce
- 2 cups diced tomatoes
- 1 cup finely sliced red capsicum
- 1 cup grated dairy-free cheese
- ½ cup coriander, chopped, to garnish

DIRECTIONS

1. Finely chop the mushrooms into tiny cubes. Grind the walnuts into a coarse crumb and set aside.
2. In a saucepan, heat olive oil over medium heat.
3. Fry the onion, garlic, and chili flakes for 5 minutes, until the onion is translucent.
4. Add the chopped mushrooms and fry for a further 5 minutes, stirring occasionally, until they begin to soften.
5. Stir in the taco seasoning and ½ cup water and simmer for 30 seconds.
6. Stir the lentils into the mushroom mixture, along with the ground walnuts.
7. Cook while stirring, for 2 minutes; until the mixture thickens.
8. Remove from heat and keep warm until ready to serve.
9. Heat the taco shells according to the packet instructions.
10. Place all the taco toppings in separate bowls, including the hot lentil and walnut filling, and the hot taco shells.

NUTRITION

Calories: 280.7 Kcal , Fat: 15.28 g , Carbohydrate: 27.15 g
Protein: 8.53 g

TEMPEH & PESTO WRAPS

| 10 min | 10 min | 4 |

INGREDIENTS

Tempeh:
- 1 portion/packet tempeh, cut into strips
- 1 clove of garlic, minced
- 1 bunch chives, finely sliced
- 2 tablespoons extra virgin olive oil
- Salt & pepper to taste

Pesto:
- 1 bunch basil
- 50g pine nuts
- 30ml extra virgin olive oil
- 1 tablespoon nutritional yeast flakes

- Salt & pepper

Wrap:
- 1 packet of your favorite wraps
- 1 punnet alfalfa sprouts
- 1 red or pink cabbage
- 2 tablespoons vegan mayo
- ½ lemon, juice only
- 3 spins of the pepper grinder

DIRECTIONS

1. Mix garlic, chives, olive oil, and salt and pepper in a bowl, and then add in the tempeh to marinate. Leave in the fridge for as long as possible.
2. Steam till tender for 7 minutes.
3. While the tempeh is steaming, make the pesto.
4. Add pine nuts and salt to the mortar and pestle, then grind to a paste.
5. Add the basil and grind, and finally add the nutritional yeast flakes, and grind one more time to a fine pulp.
6. Stir in the olive oil to create a nice paste and set aside.
7. Set 4 wraps onto plates and spread the alfalfa sprouts onto the wraps.
8. In a separate bowl, shred the red cabbage and pour in the mayo, lemon juice, and pepper — mix until combined.
9. Place this cabbage slaw on top of the sprouts.
10. Add warm tempeh and spoonfuls of pesto.

NUTRITION

Calories: 145.5 Kcal , Fat: 10.1 g , Carbohydrates: 5.04 g
Protein: 6.42 g

MUSHROOM RAGU LASAGNA WITH CELERIAC BÉCHAMEL

| 40 min | 1 Hr | 8 |

INGREDIENTS

- 1 packet vegan lasagna sheets
- Extra virgin olive oil
- Salt

Ragu:
- 100g Swiss brown mushrooms
- 4g salt
- 50ml vegetable oil
- 1 leek, diced
- 1 red capsicum, diced
- 1 long red chili,
- 3 sprigs thyme
- 1 stalk celery, diced
- 1 carrot, diced

- 1 onion, diced
- 2 bay leaves
- 3 sprigs thyme
- 3 cloves garlic, sliced
- 300g mixed mushrooms
- 30g dried shiitake mushrooms
- 1 tablespoon tomato paste
- 100ml red wine
- 1 x (400g) can cherry tomatoes
- 300ml vegetable stock

- ½ teaspoon smoked paprika
- Bunch parsley stalks, roughly chopped

Plant-Based Bèchamel:
- 1 celeriac
- 300ml oat milk
- 2 tablespoons nutritional yeast
- ¼ teaspoon salt
- Thyme

Breadcrumbs:
- 200g breadcrumbs
- 2 cloves garlic
- 3 sprigs thyme

DIRECTIONS

You can make it the ultimate comfort food. The lasagna uses a deceiving version of mushroom soy sauce to give it that extra umami flavor.

Preheat the oven to 180C.
Make the mushroom soy sauce.
Pound up the Swiss brown mushroom in a food processor with some salt.
Spoon into a bowl and leave it for as long as it takes to make the rest of the ingredients.
Place a large saucepan on medium-low heat.
Add the vegetable oil, capsicum, and leek, red chili with the seeds removed, celery, bay leaves, carrot, onion, garlic, and thyme.
Place into the pan and cook for 10 minutes; until the onions have become translucent.
Dice up the mixed mushrooms and throw them in the pan.
Blend the dried shiitake to a powder
Add that in too. Cook the mushrooms until the liquid has been cooked out.
Put red wine, vegetable stock, smoked paprika, parsley stalks, a tin of cherry tomatoes, and tomato paste.
Squeeze the juice out of the salted mushrooms into the pot.
Reserve the mushrooms till the end and keep cooking on medium heat until the liquid has been cooked out again.
Cook over low heat for 40 minutes; until the mixture has reduced.
Peel the celeriac and chop into small-inch-sized bits.
Add them to a saucepan with oat milk, nutritional yeast, and salt and pepper.
Cook until it has gone super soft.
Remove the bay leaves and thyme stalks and beat them into a smooth paste.
Mix the breadcrumbs with thyme and minced garlic.
Lay a scoop of the mushroom ragu at the bottom of a baking tray.
Lay some lasagna sheets on top then more mushroom, add the béchamel then pasta sheets.
Repeat until you run out of either space, pasta sheets, or ragu.
Top the béchamel with the garlic bread crumb mixture.
Drizzle a small amount of olive oil to help the breadcrumbs go crispy, and top with a pinch of salt.
Cover with foil and bake in the oven for 20 minutes
Remove the foil and continue baking for another 20 minutes; until the top is roasted golden and bubbling away.
Allow sitting for 45 minutes before serving.

NUTRITION

Calories: 122.5 Kcal , Carbohydrates: 6.66 g , Fat: 5.67 g
Proteins: 15.65 g

COCONUT CHERRY TRUFFLES

20 min	5 min	16

INGREDIENTS

- 2 cups shredded coconut
- 2 teaspoons pure vanilla extract
- ¼ teaspoon salt
- 4 tablespoons coconut oil, melted
- 3 tablespoons agave syrup
- 2 tablespoons full-cream coconut milk
- 75 g glacé cherries, roughly chopped
- A drop of red food coloring (optional)
- 300 g dairy-free dark chocolate

DIRECTIONS

Something is calming in making a treat that looks satisfying and pricy and that costs a small fortune.

1. Line a baking tray with baking paper.
2. Place coconut, vanilla, and salt in a blender.
3. Pour in the agave syrup, coconut milk, and coconut oil.
4. Beat in until the mixture is very roughly combined.
5. Spoon the mixture out of the blender, into a mixing bowl.
6. Mix to ensure vanilla, coconut milk, and oil are uniformly distributed.
7. Divide the mixture into two even portions.
8. To one portion, add the cherries and red food coloring, if using.
9. Roll the mixtures into teaspoon-sized balls and put them on the baking tray.
10. Pop the tray in the fridge for not less than 30 minutes to allow the coconut filling to set.
11. Once the coconut centers are cold, melt the chocolate, either in the microwave or in a double boiler on your stovetop.
12. Remove from the heat.
13. Drop one coconut ball into the chocolate and roll to cover.
14. Scoop it out with a fork and allow any excess chocolate to drip off before placing it back on the baking tray.
15. Place the tray back in the fridge to set the chocolate once you've choc-dipped all your truffles.

NUTRITION

Calories: 5.65 Kcal , Fat: 0.35 g , Carbohydrate: 0.57 g
Protein: 0.09 g

VEGAN FRIED SHRIMPS

16 min	20 min	4

INGREDIENTS

- Fried vegan shrimp:
- 14 ounces can heart of palm drained (7.7 ounces drained weight)
- 3 Tablespoons all-purpose flour
- ¼ cup non-dairy milk
- ½ cup panko breadcrumbs
- 1 teaspoon Old Bay seasoning and an extra
- couple of shakes
- Organic canola oil for shallow frying
- Cocktail sauce:
- ¼ cup ketchup
- 1 teaspoon prepared horse radish
- ½ teaspoon hot sauce
- ⅛ teaspoon vegan Worces tershire sauce optional

DIRECTIONS

Need something fancy for a family dinner? Vegan fried shrimp is perfect as an appetizer or entrée. Creatively making the hearts of palm, cut into bite-sized pieces, breaded in seasoned panko breadcrumbs, and fried until beautifully crisped. Toss it up with a cocktail sauce for dipping.

Course: Appetizer

Fried vegan shrimp:

Dry the hearts of the palm on a clean kitchen towel by patting them.

Move the hearts of the palm to a cutting board; cut them into 1-inch-long pieces. To a dinner plate, put 2 Tablespoons of flour.

For the remaining flour, add to a bowl containing non-dairy milk.

Use a fork to evenly combine it and get out any lumps.

To a plate with 1/2 teaspoon of Old Bay seasoning, add 1/4 cup of panko breadcrumbs.

Mix the seasoning throughout the breadcrumbs with your fingers; they will evenly distribute.

Bring a non-stick skillet to medium-high heat with about a half-inch of organic canola oil before breading the hearts of palm.

Bread the hearts of palm as the oil heats. Roll a piece of the heart of the palm in the flour until it's covered; one at a time. Dip the heart of palm into the mixture of milk and then gently tap it on its side to remove any excess flour.

Roll in seasoned panko breadcrumbs. While breading the hearts of palm, add 1/4 cup on the plate with an additional 1/2 teaspoon or so of the Old Bay seasoning.

Put the breaded hearts of palm on a clean plate and continue this process until all of the pieces are breaded.

Put the hearts of the palm into the oil and fry for 4 minutes, rotating the hearts of the palm as they brown to ensure every part is fried.

Move the hearts of the palm once browned to a clean, towel-lined plate to drain.

Top more Old Bay seasoning on the breaded hearts of palm

Serve with cocktail sauce.

Slowly cut into the side of a few of the breaded and fried hearts of palm so that they can be served lined around the rim of a cocktail glass. But be careful to not cut all the way through.

Then put the cocktail sauce into the glass and place the vegan shrimp on the side through the slits.

Cocktail sauce:

Combine ketchup in a small bowl, hot sauce, and vegan Worcestershire sauce, 1/2 teaspoon prepared horseradish, if using.

Taste and add 1/2 teaspoon of prepared horseradish if you'd like a more pungent flavor.

NUTRITION

Calories: 289.5 Kcal , Fat: 8.28 g , Carbohydrates: 83.82 g
Protein: 13.07 g

CHICKPEA SALAD

10 min   0 min   2

INGREDIENTS

Salad:
- 8 ounces of vegan Mozzarella
- 1 cup drained chickpeas
- ½ cup chopped grape tomatoes
- ½ cup chopped cucumbers
- 1 chopped small handful of fresh dill
- ½ cup chopped grape tomatoes
- ½ cup sliced vegan prosciutto
- Salt and pepper to taste

Vinaigrette:
- 2 teaspoons honey
- 3 tablespoons extra virgin olive oil
- ⅓ lemon juice
- 1 teaspoon balsamic vinegar
- salt and pepper to taste

DIRECTIONS

1. Drain the vegan mozzarella and put it into a large bowl
2. Wash and drain the chickpeas.
3. Cut the tomatoes, cucumbers.
4. Add to the bowl containing the vegan mozzarella.
5. Chop fresh dill and add to the bowl.
6. Pour the vinaigrette over the salad and gently but carefully toss.
7. Dress with salt, fresh dill, broccoli flowers, and pepper

NUTRITION

Carbohydrate: 27 g , Fat: 9 g , Protein: 10 g , Calories: 305 Kcal

---

GREEN PASTA PRIMAVERA

15 min   15 min   6

INGREDIENTS

- ½ chopped broccoli head
- Kosher salt and freshly ground black pepper
- 1 chopped leek
- 1 pound of favorite pasta
- 2 tablespoons freshly squeezed lemon juice
- 4 thinly sliced scallions
- 2 thinly sliced green garlic stalks
- 3 minced garlic cloves
- 1 bunch chopped parsley
- 1 handful thinly sliced green beans or green peas
- 2 teaspoons grated lemon zest
- 2 cups grated vegan Parmesan cheese
- ¼ cup extra-virgin olive oil

DIRECTIONS

1. Bring water to a boil and add a couple of big pinches of salt.
2. Cook the pasta until oven ready.
3. Keep 2 cups of pasta water.
4. Strain the pasta.
5. Heat the oil in a large saucepan over medium heat.
6. Add the leek, scallions, and garlic.
7. Cook for 3 minutes, until they soften slightly.
8. Add the broccoli and green beans to the pan. Season with salt and pepper.
9. Cook for 7 minutes until they are tender.
10. 10. Add the lemon zest, cooked pasta, grated vegan Parmesan cheese, lemon juice, and 1 cup of pasta water to the vegetables.
11. Stir everything together and cook for 5 minutes over medium-low heat; it should be visibly thicker and creamy.
12. Add more pasta water as needed and take the pan off heat then mix in the parsley.
13. Serve with oil or butter on top.

NUTRITION

Calories: 190 Kcal , Fat: 10 g , Carbohydrate: 21 g , Protein: 4 g

SPAGHETTI ALL'UBRIACO

| 20 min | 15 min | 4 |

INGREDIENTS

- Coarse sea salt
- 340 grams of dried spaghett
- ⅛ teaspoon freshly grated nutmeg
- ½ teaspoon red pepper flakes
- 60 milliliters extra-virgin olive oil
- 45 grams finely chopped nuts
- 4 thinly sliced small garlic cloves
- ⅛ teaspoon freshly grated nutmeg
- 1 cup of 250 milliliters red wine
- 1.6 ounces or 45 grams freshly grated Pecorino Romano cheese
- Fine sea salt
- Freshly ground black pepper
- ⅛ teaspoon freshly grated nutmeg

DIRECTIONS

This version is made with nuts, red pepper flakes, herbs, and garlic. You can use fewer cloves in place of garlic and clone with red pepper flakes.

1. Put three-quarters of water into a pot and bring it to a boil over medium-high heat.
2. Add a generous amount of coarse salt.
3. Cook the spaghetti for 2 minutes until oven ready. Don't rely on the package instructions.
4. Heat the olive oil in a large, high-sided pan over medium-low heat while the pasta is cooking.
5. Add the garlic and red pepper flakes.
6. Cook while stirring, for 1 minute; until the garlic is fragrant.
7. Pour the wine into the pan with the garlic and stir.
8. Remove from the heat while the pasta finishes cooking.
9. Drain the pasta, reserving 250 milliliters of the pasta water.
10. Add the pasta to the pan containing wine and garlic
11. Turn the pan to medium heat and stir.
12. Let it cook as you gently stir for 2 minutes; until the pasta is oven-ready and has absorbed most of the wine.
13. Remove the pan from the heat and mix in the nuts.
14. Stir in a tablespoon of the reserved pasta water.
15. Finish with the nutmeg and season with salt and pepper.
16. Stir to incorporate well.
17. Taste and adjust the seasoning.
18. Serve graced with parsley.

NUTRITION

Calories: 173 kcal , Carbohydrate: 37.2 g , Fat: 0.8 g , Protein: 7.5 g Sodium: 4.2 mg

MISO-GARLIC SNAP PEA SALAD

| 30 min | 15 min | 4 |

INGREDIENTS

- 2 teaspoons white miso
- 3 tablespoons extra-virgin olive oil
- 1 small grated and minced garlic clove
- 1 tablespoon of lemon zest
- 2 tablespoons of lemon juice
- ¼ cup grated vegan pecorino
- 1 can of drained and rinsed chickpeas
- 2 sliced scallions (light green and white parts)
- 1 pound snap peas
- ½ cup roughly chopped fresh mint leaves and tender stems
- Kosher salt and freshly cracked black pepper
- 1 teaspoon white or black sesame seeds

DIRECTIONS

1. In a serving bowl, whisk the garlic, lemon juice and zest, olive oil, and miso. Make sure they are smooth, and the miso has dissolved.
2. Add the chickpeas, scallions, snap peas, and grated vegan pecorino, rolling to mix.
3. Season with salt and pepper to taste.
4. To serve, you can top with mint, sesame seeds, and vegan pecorino.
5. Serve.

NUTRITION

Calories: 231.12 Kcal , Fat: 8.77 g , Carbohydrate: 30.93 g Protein: 9.77 g

MACADAMIA-COCONUT PANNA COTTA

| 1Hr 15 min | 15 min | 6 |

INGREDIENTS

Macadamia-Coconut Panna Cotta:
- 1 vanilla bean with seeds scraped and pod reserved
- 3 cups filtered water; divided into 1 tablespoon
- 1 cup dried coconut (unsweetened shredded)
- Pinch sea salt
- Small strawberries with stems
- 4 teaspoons agar-agar flakes
- 1 teaspoon agar powder
- 1 cup macadamia nuts (raw)
- Macerated strawberries, for serving

- 2 tablespoons light maple syrup
- 1 teaspoon arrowroot powder
- 1 tablespoon vanilla extract

Macerated Strawberries:
- 1 teaspoon vanilla extract
- 2 cups or 230 grams small hulled and quartered fresh strawberries
- 1 tablespoon maple syrup

DIRECTIONS

Panna cotta is an Italian word that translates to "cooked cream." Traditionally, gelatin is dissolved in warm cream to give it a desirable mouthfeel.
This is a vegan recipe without cream or gelatin but with a rich texture and flavor.

1. Put 3 cups of water, coconut, macadamia nuts, and salt into a food processer. Blend on high speed until completely smooth.
2. Pour through the nut milk bag into the bowl.
3. Squeeze the bag to extract as much milk as possible. This should give you 3 cups. If it doesn't, remove some and add more water until you've reached 3 cups.
4. Compost the nut pulp left in the bag.
5. Pour the macadamia-coconut milk into a medium pot and whisk in the vanilla bean pod, scraped seeds, agar-agar, and maple syrup.
6. Bring to a boil over medium-high heat, while whisking.
7. Cover the pot and reduce the heat to low.
8. Simmer for 10 minutes; until no agar-agar flakes are visible.
9. Dissolve the arrowroot in the remaining tablespoon of water and slowly drizzle into the simmering milk mixture.
10. Once the mixture returns to a boil, remove it from heat.
11. Remove the vanilla bean pod and compost and reserve for another use.
12. Add the vanilla extract and whisk again.
13. Divide the mixture between 6 small or medium-sized bowls and leave for 15 minutes.
14. Carefully place the bowls in the fridge to set completely, at least 1 hour or up to 2 days ahead.
15. Combine the maple, strawberries, and vanilla in a medium bowl and gently toss when ready to serve.
16. Set aside for not less than 10 minutes to allow the strawberries to macerate.
17. Serve the panna cotta cold, each topped with a spoonful of strawberries and a whole fresh strawberry.

NUTRITION

Calories: 220 Kcal , Carbohydrate: 28 g , Fat: 11.7 g , Protein: 2.0 g

FRENCH ONION SOUP WITH ASPARAGUS

| 25 min | 1 Hr | 6 |

INGREDIENTS

- 4 tablespoons extra-virgin olive oil
- 2 ½ pounds halved and thinly sliced onions
- Freshly ground black pepper
- ⅓ cup dry vermouth
- 2 ounces shredded white Cheddar
- 3 tablespoons white wine vinegar
- 2 tablespoons water

- ½ tablespoon vegan Worcestershire sauce
- 7 ounces crusty bread.
- 10 ounces trimmed

DIRECTIONS

1. Heat 3 tablespoons of olive oil over medium heat.
2. Stir in the onions and season with a couple of big pinches of salt and pepper.
3. Cook, while occasionally stirring every 5 or so minutes, until the onions are soft and deeply caramelized.
4. Add water to the pot to remove onions that are stuck at the bottom of the pot.
5. Add water and reduce the heat to medium-low if you find the onions are looking charred or fried instead of soft and golden.
6. Stir in the vermouth and leave to cook for 2 minutes
7. Stir in the Worcestershire and add 8 cups of water.
8. Season with more salt and pepper and turn up the heat to high.
9. Bring the mixture to a boil, then reduce and simmer for 20 minutes.
10. Taste the soup and season with more salt and pepper.
11. Heat the oven to 375°F while the soup is simmering.
12. Toss the torn bread with the remaining 1 tablespoon olive oil and season lightly with salt and pepper.
13. Bake for 20 minutes, tossing halfway through, until golden and crispy.
14. Remove the bread and sprinkle over the cheese.
15. Return the pan to the oven and bake until the vegan cheese melts for about 3 minutes.
16. Stir in the asparagus to the soup before serving.
17. Serve the soup topped with cheesy croutons and black pepper.

NUTRITION

Calories: 120 , Carbohydrate: 13 g , Fat: 6 g , Protein: 3 g
Sodium: 590 mg

VEGAN CURRY WITH VEGETABLES

30 min   1Hr 30min   8

INGREDIENTS

- 3 tied into knots pandan leaves
- 10 pieces of rinsed in hot water and halved fried tofu puffs
- 5 slices galangal
- 1 ¼ cups neutral oil
- 2 small eggplants
- 8 ounces roughly chopped red jalapeños
- 4 garlic cloves
- 2 stalks of lemongrass with white parts roughly chopped and green parts discarded
- 2 teaspoons ground cumin
- 1 teaspoon ground turmeric
- 2 teaspoons ground coriander
- 7 cups vegetable stock

- 4 ounces sliced okra (tips removed)
- 1 cup coconut milk
- 1 roughly chopped shallot
- 3 cups roughly chopped cabbage
- 2 cut into wedges tomatoes
- 5 lime leaves with stems removed and thinly sliced
- 5 curry leaves
- 1 ½ palm roughly chopped sugar rounds
- 2 teaspoons kosher salt
- ¼ teaspoon mushrooms seasoning or vegetable bouillon
- 1 tablespoon lime juice
- 1 tablespoon tamarind juice

DIRECTIONS

This recipe is made from shallot, red jalapenos, lemongrass, garlic, and galangal. The paste is sautéed for 30 minutes until aromatized and later simmered with tomatoes, tofu puffs, eggplant, cabbage, and okra.

1. In a saucepan heat 1 cup of oil to 350°F.
2. Fry the eggplant sticks for 2 minutes; until the skin turns slightly darker and transfers to paper towels using a pair of tongs to drain.
3. Put water into another saucepan and bring to a boil.
4. Blanch the okra for 1 minute then drain and set aside.
5. For the chile paste, put the jalapeños, galangal, shallot, garlic, lemongrass, and 2 tablespoons of oil in a food processor.
6. Blend into a fine paste.
7. Heat the oven over medium-low heat
8. Add the remaining 2 tablespoons of oil, and pan-fry the chile paste, stirring periodically, until it turns to a darker shade of red.
9. Add more oil to avoid the pan getting dry along the way.
10. Add the coriander, cumin, and turmeric.
11. Continue to pan-fry until fragrant.
12. Add the stock, pandan, and tofu.
13. Bring to a boil.
14. Cover the pot and leave it to simmer for 10 minutes under medium-low heat.
15. Uncover the pot after 10 minutes.
16. Add the cabbage, lime leaves, tomatoes, eggplant, and curry leaves while the broth is simmering.
17. Immerse the vegetables in the broth with the help of a spatula if it is necessary.
18. Spice with palm sugar, salt, and mushrooms.
19. Adjust the seasoning if needed.
20. Once the cabbage is crispy and tender, add the okra and coconut milk, then simmer for 3 minutes.
21. Whirl in the lime juice, taste, and adjust the seasoning if needed.
22. Remove the pandan leaves before serving.

NUTRITION

Calories: 180 , Carbohydrate: 28 g , Fat: 7 g , Protein: 3 g
Sodium: 820

VEGAN ZUCCHINI FRITTERS WITH CUCUMBER RAITA

0 min   0 min   3

INGREDIENTS

Fritters:
- 2 cups of grated zucchini
- 3 cloves minced garlic
- 2 tablespoons coconut oil
- ½ cup grated onion
- ½ cup cornmeal
- 1 teaspoon cumin
- 2 cups chopped spinach
- 1 can chickpeas
- pinch salt and pepper

Indian Cucumber Salad:
- 1 cup finely chopped English cucumber
- 1 cup vegan plain yogurt
- ½ teaspoon cumin
- 1 teaspoon fresh dill
- 1 clove of pressed garlic
- ¼ teaspoon cayenne
- Salt

DIRECTIONS

Fritters:
1. Heat a frying pan over medium heat.
2. Add coconut oil, onion, zucchini, and garlic.
3. Panfry for 4 minutes, stirring until soft.
4. Add spinach until withered for 3 minutes.
5. Strain and gently dry with a paper towel to remove any excess water.
6. Add chickpeas and mash with a potato masher or the back of a fork until your chickpeas are uniform in a large mixing bowl.
7. Add sautéed veggies, cornmeal, and seasoning.
8. Get in with your hands to produce a well-combined mixture.
9. Add more cornmeal as needed.
10. Form into 1-inch-thick by 4 diameter patties.
11. Add oil to the pan over medium-high heat.
12. Add in your fritters without crowding.
13. Fry until brown for 4 minutes on each side.

Cucumber Raita:
14. Add all the ingredients for the Cucumber Raita in a bowl.
15. Top raita over the fritters.
16. Serve!

NUTRITION

Calories: 111.6 Kcal , Carbohydrate: 27.9 g

VEGAN SPRING PEA AND MUNG BEAN FRITTERS

0 min	20 min	4

INGREDIENTS

Fritters:
- ½ cup mung flour
- ½ cup chickpea flour
- 4 finely chopped spring onions
- 2 tablespoons lemon juice
- 3 cups fresh or frozen spring peas
- 2 tablespoons tahini
- 2 tablespoons olive oil
- 2 tablespoons lemon zest
- 2 tablespoons finely chopped cilantro
- 1 teaspoon ground coriander
- 1 teaspoon salt
- 2 teaspoons frying sunflower oil
- Fresh greens, for garnish

Herbed Yogurt Sauce:
- ½ cup plain organic coconut yogurt
- 1 teaspoon lemon zest
- ½ teaspoon ground coriander
- 1 tablespoon finely chopped cilantro
- ⅛ teaspoon salt

DIRECTIONS

Fritters:
1. Put water into a medium pot and bring to a boil.
2. Blanch the peas for 4 minutes.
3. Drain the peas through a sieve.
4. Dry off the excess water.
5. Reserve 1 cup of peas and put the remaining in a food processor.
6. Throb a few times until the mixture breaks and forms a thick paste.
7. Repeat to incorporate the remaining cup of peas and to add texture.
8. Add in more flour; 1 spoonful at a go to ensure the mixture isn't too wet.
9. Portion out the patties with an ice cream scoop.
10. Shape into balls about 2 inches wide with your wet hands and flatten into 3/4-inch-thick disks.
11. Heat sunflower oil; 1 teaspoon, on medium heat, in a well-seasoned frying pan.
12. Fry the fritters for 3 minutes, until they are golden and crispy on each side.
13. Flip the fritters with a greased spatula.
14. Cook only 2 at a time to avoid overcrowding in the pan.
15. Place the fritters on a plate lined with a paper towel to absorb the oil.
16. Serve when still hot with fresh greens and a spoonful of the yogurt sauce.

Herbed Yogurt:
17. Mix all ingredients in a bowl until well combined.
18. Taste and adjust flavors as desired.

Mung flour:
19. Blend 1 cup of the mung beans in a blender.
20. Be sure to store the flour in a sealed container until ready to use.

NUTRITION

Calories: 140 Kcal , Carbohydrate: 10.7 g , Fat: 9 g , Protein: 4.2 g

---

VEGAN SPINACH ARTICHOKE DIP

0 min	20 min	6

INGREDIENTS

- 1 cup raw cashews
- 4 cloves finely chopped garlic
- 1 medium-sized finely chopped, onion
- 2 teaspoons of coconut oil
- 1 can of chopped artichoke hearts both strained and pat dry
- ¼ cup nutritional yeast
- 1 ¼ cups unsweetened almond milk
- 5 ounces baby spinach
- 1 tablespoon lemon juice
- 2 teaspoons miso
- ¾ teaspoon sea salt
- ½ teaspoon pepper

DIRECTIONS

1. Pre-heat oven to 375°F.
2. Add raw cashews to a bowl and add boiling water over top and leave to soak.
3. Add the garlic, onion, and coconut oil to a medium-sized skillet.
4. Bring to medium heat and cook until softened.
5. Add the baby spinach and cook until wilted.
6. Add the artichoke hearts and simmer to remove any excess water.
7. Add strained cashews to a high-speed blender with almond milk, miso, salt nutritional yeast, lemon juice, and pepper.
8. Blend until smooth.
9. Add the cooked spinach and artichoke and throb a few times for a chunky texture.
10. Transfer the mixture to a medium-sized baking dish.
11. Cook for 20 minutes; until the dip becomes aromatic and starts to brown around the edges.
12. Leave to cool slightly.
13. Slowly mix with a spoon to expose the soft interior.
14. Serve with toasted baguette, gluten-free crackers, or nachos chips.

NUTRITION

Calories: 127.98 Kcal , Carbohydrate: 25.92 g , Fat: 0.16g Protein: 5.83 g

CHICKPEA TUNA SALAD SANDWICH

INGREDIENTS

- 15 ounces can of rinsed and drained chickpeas
- 3 stalks finely chopped celery with leaves
- 2 teaspoons kelp flakes
- ½ teaspoon each of the onion powder, dill, parsley, celery salt, and Old Bay seasoning
- 2 tablespoons unsweetened dill pickle relish
- ¼ teaspoon black pepper
- 2 tablespoons vegan mayonnaise

DIRECTIONS

This dish is made out of chickpeas and seaweed flakes to give it a taste and scent of tuna and it contains plenty of protein.

1. Mash the chickpeas in a bowl. Add all ingredients and mix.
2. Add more flakes if you want it to taste like the sea
3. Refrigerate until ready to serve.
4. Serve on a platter with lettuce and veggies or put it in a sandwich.

NUTRITION

Calories: 447 , Fat: 24 g , Protein: 19 g , Sodium: 1874 g

VEGAN 'TUNA' CASSEROLE

INGREDIENTS

- 1 kg whole wheat noodles
- 3 tablespoons oat flour
- 1 tablespoon oil
- 2 tablespoons vegan butter
- 1 kg vegan cheese shreds
- 1 ½ cup almond milk
- 1 tablespoon minced garlic
- 1 tablespoon Dijon mustard
- 1 kg thawed and frozen cauliflower
- 2 jars drained sliced mushrooms
- 1 can vegan tuna
- ¼ kg kiwi vegetable chip mix
- ½ kg vegan cheddar shreds

DIRECTIONS

To make this dish, you'll need a combination of vegan butter, oat flour, almond milk, and homemade macaroni to give you that look, texture, and flavor.

1. Turn oven to 350 degrees.
2. Turn a large pot of water on high and pour in noodles when water is boiling.
3. Add teaspoon salt and Stir.
4. Turn on medium-high heat to the smaller pot.
5. Add oil, butter, and flour and whisk for 1 minute.
6. Add milk and whisk until thickened for 3 minutes.
7. Add garlic and mustard.
8. Add vegan cheese shreds and whisk until melted.
9. Drain pasta and pour into the pot.
10. Put the vegan cheese, mushrooms, tuna, and cauliflower.
11. Stir until combined then pour into baking dish.
12. Crush chips and sprinkle over top of the mixture.
13. Spread half the bag of vegan cheddar shreds over the chips and bake for 20 minutes.
14. Serve.

NUTRITION

Calories: 250 Kcal , Fat: 23 g , Protein: 12 g

LOBSTER MUSHROOM BISQUE

0 min	30 min	4

INGREDIENTS

- 1 cup-soaked raw cashews
- 1 tablespoon cornstarch
- 1 cup vegetable broth
- 1 tablespoon kelp powder
- 1 minced shallot
- 3 garlic cloves
- 1 tablespoon olive oil
- ½ cup diced carrots
- ½ cup celery, diced
- 3 tablespoons tomato paste
- 1 teaspoon smoked paprika
- 4 cups vegetable broth
- 1 cup white wine
- 2 cups dried soaked lobster mushrooms
- 1 bay leaf
- 1 teaspoon thyme
- ¼ teaspoon cayenne
- Salt and pepper

DIRECTIONS

This lobster mushroom bisque dish is creamy and warm sea-food-free. You can achieve this rich dish with creamy cashews and blended veggies.

1. Soak cashews for 3 hours or up to overnight.
2. Take the soaked cashews and add them to a blender with 1 cup of vegetable broth, kelp powder, and cornstarch.
3. Blend until smooth. Set aside.
4. Soak the Lobster mushrooms, for a few minutes until they are soft.
5. Add olive oil and heat on medium in a large soup pot.
6. Add shallot, garlic, carrot, and celery to the pot
7. Cook for 4 minutes until they begin to soften.
8. Add the tomato paste into the vegetables and stir.
9. Add the wine, broth, mushroom, wine, and cashew cream mixture.
10. Add the rest of the seasonings.
11. Bring to a soft boil and reduce to low heat and cook for 10 minutes to develop flavor and finish cooking everything.
12. Add salt and pepper to taste and adjust flavoring as you need it.
13. Serve.

NUTRITION

Calories: 291 Kcal , Fat: 15 g , Protein: 8 g , Sodium: 1310 mg

---

UNSMOKED SALMON SCRAMBLE

0 min	20 min	2

INGREDIENTS

Smoked salmon:
- 4 carrots
- 1 tablespoon lemon juice
- 1 tablespoon olive oil
- smoked salt
- 1 handful chopped fresh fennel
- Pinch cracked black pepper

Scramble:
- 1 block plain tofu
- 2 tsp tamari
- 1 tsp turmeric
- 1 large finely chopped onion
- 2 cloves finely chopped garlic
- Olive oil
- Black pepper
- Sea salt to taste

DIRECTIONS

Smoked Salmon:
1. Thinly slice the carrots using a mandolin and put them in a bowl
2. To the carrots, add olive oil, lemon juice, fennel, smoked salt, and pepper; and mix well.
3. Cover with cling film and leave to marinate overnight in the refrigerator.
4. Smoke the carrots using a cold smoker or over coals.

Scramble:
5. Squeeze out excess water in the tofu and crumble in a bowl
6. Add the turmeric and tamari and mix
7. Lightly pan-fry the onion and garlic. Be sure not to overcook them.
8. Add the tofu mixture and heat everything through while stirring continuously.

Assembling:
9. Toast some vegan health bread.
10. Gently heap some of the scrambles on top.
11. Add a few slivers of the smoked carrots
12. Grace with a sprig or two of fennel tops.

NUTRITION

Calories: 447 Kcal , Carbohydrate: 54 g , Fat: 24 g , Protein: 19 g
Sodium: 1874 g , Sugar: 2 g

VEGAN GEFILTE FISH

| 0 min | 0 min | 4 |

INGREDIENTS

- 1 tablespoon extra-virgin olive oil
- ½ small, chopped onion
- 1 large, chopped celery stalk
- 1 large, chopped carrot
- 2 cloves garlic, chopped
- 15 ounces can of drained and rinsed chickpeas
- Salt and black pepper
- 1 tablespoon Old Bay seasoning
- 1 ½ tablespoon dulse flakes
- 1 tablespoon kelp flakes
- ⅛ tablespoon cayenne pepper
- 1 lemon Zest and juice
- Red shredded cabbage
- Prepared horseradish

DIRECTIONS

1. Put oil on a frying pan and heat over medium-high heat.
2. Add the carrots, onion, celery, and garlic.
3. Let the seamer for 4 minutes.
4. Add the chickpeas to the frying pan.
5. Toss with the veggies.
6. Add in the seasonings.
7. Take it out of the heat and leave to cool.
8. Transfer the chickpeas and veggie mixture to a food processor.
9. Add the lemon zest and half lemon juice extracted from the lemon.
10. Throb the mixture and process until smooth.
11. Taste for and adjust any seasonings if necessary.
12. Scoop 1/3 cup of the mixture and mold into a gefilte fish shape.
13. Lay the molded gefilte "fish" on a plate.
14. Do the same for the remaining mixture.
15. Cover the gefilte fishes with plastic wrap.
16. Refrigerate for not less than an hour; until ready to serve.
17. Serve the pieces on a small bed of red cabbage.
18. Season with a small slice or a few shreds of carrot.
19. Squeeze the lemon juice over the "fish" and cabbage.
20. Serve and enjoy your gefilte fish.

NUTRITION

Calories: 194 Kcal , Carbohydrate: 33 g , Fat: 5 g , Protein: 7 g
Sodium: 315 mg , Sugar: 10 g

COCONUT-CRUSTED FISHLESS STICKS

| | 35 min | |

INGREDIENTS

Fishless fingers:
- 14 ounces can of hearts of palm
- ½ teaspoon garlic powder
- 1 tablespoon white wine vinegar
- ½ teaspoon sea salt
- ½ cup brown rice flour
- ½ cup non-dairy milk
- ½ cup desiccated coconut
- ¼ cup cornflour

Dill mayonnaise:
- ¼ cup vegan mayonnaise
- 2 tablespoons chopped fresh dill
- 1 tablespoon capers

DIRECTIONS

Fishless Fingers:
1. Preheat the oven to 375°F
2. Prepare a baking tray with parchment paper.
3. Drain the tin of palm of hearts and transfer them to a bowl.
4. Tear the hearts into thin stringy pieces and rip them apart using two forks.
5. Add sea salt, garlic powder, and 2 tablespoons brown rice flour and stir
6. Add the brown rice flour to a shallow bowl.
7. Take another shallow bowl and add non-dairy milk and whisk in the cornflour.
8. Take a third bowl and add the coconut.
9. Put a heaped tablespoon of the palm of heart mixture, one after the other, and roll into a sausage shape.
10. Flatten slightly into a fish finger-like shape.
11. Coat in the brown rice flour and dip into the milk mixture
12. Add the coconut.
13. Place this onto your lined baking tray.
14. Repeat until the mixture has been used.
15. Place in the oven for 30 minutes; until golden brown.
Dill Mayo:
16. Whisk all the ingredients and transfer to a small dipping bowl while the fish filets cook. (Whisk them together)
17. Wait until you are ready to serve.

NUTRITION

Calories: 291 , Carbs: 27 g , Fat: 15 g , Protein: 8 g
Sodium: 1310 mg , Sugar: 6 g

VEGAN SALMON PATTIES

| 0 min | 0 min | 5 |

INGREDIENTS

- 2 ⅓ cup grated carrot
- 4 chopped tomatoes
- ½ finely grated peel and juice lemon
- 1 tablespoon white vinegar
- 1 pinch of sea salt
- 2 tablespoons vegetable oil
- 3 tablespoons chopped fresh dill
- 12 ounces soy
- 4 tablespoons vegan mayonnaise
- grated horseradish
- 4 tablespoons vegan caviar

DIRECTIONS

1. Mix the grated carrot, soy "meat", lemon peel, chopped tomatoes, lemon juice, fresh dill, salt, white vinegar, and oil.
2. Put the mixture in a baking dish and bake at 300 F, until carrot softens. That should take about 25 minutes.
3. Form patties and put a spoonful of black Caviar and a slice of lemon on top.
4. Mix grated horseradish with mayonnaise.
5. Serve the patties with the mayo mixture and boiled or baked potatoes.
6. Grace with a lemon slice and a sprig of dill.

NUTRITION

Calories: 187 Kcal , Carbohydrate: 0.40 g , Fat: 9.07 g
Protein: 24.43 g

ROASTED SWEET POTATO SUSHI

| 15 min | 30 min | 3 |

INGREDIENTS

Roasted sweet potato filling:
- 1 large sweet potato
- 1 tablespoon vegetable oil
- 1 tablespoon sesame oil
- 1 tablespoon maple syrup

Rice:
- 1 cup sushi rice
- 1 ⅓ cups of water
- 1 ½ tablespoon rice vinegar
- ¾ tablespoon salt
- Serving:
- 2 scallions
- 3 sheets nori
- Wasabi
- Toasted sesame seeds
- Pickled ginger
- Soy sauce

DIRECTIONS

1. Preheat the oven to 375° and line a baking sheet with parchment.
2. Stir oil, maple syrup, and sesame oil in a small bowl.
3. Peel the sweet potato and cut into strips that are just under ½ inch thick.
4. Rub with oil and maple syrup mixture.
5. Place and toss into a bowl to coat and then arrange strips on a baking sheet.
6. Bake for 25 minutes, until tender, gently turning halfway through.
7. Place rice into a fine-mesh strainer and rinse under cold running water for 2 minutes while the sweet potatoes bake.
8. Place rice into a small saucepan
9. Add water, vinegar, and salt and place over high heat.
10. Stir a few times to incorporate and leave to simmer.
11. Lower heat and cover.
12. Leave to continue simmering for another 20 minutes; until all liquid is absorbed.
13. Allow sitting for 10 minutes before uncovering.
14. Place a sheet on the bamboo mat.
15. Cover nori with a thin layer of rice with wet hands.
16. Arrange your sweet potato strips in a single line along the width of nori, about one inch away from you.
17. Arrange the scallion pieces right alongside the sweet potato strips.
18. Take the ends of the bamboo mat and end of nori and tightly roll it over your fillings.
19. Tuck the end of the nori in, at the corners and continue rolling,
20. Press your roll tight with the mat.
21. After you've rolled them, slice them into eight pieces.
22. Repeat the same procedure using your remaining nori sheets and fillings.
23. Sprinkle with sesame seeds and serve with soy sauce, wasabi, and pickled ginger.

NUTRITION

Calories 456Kcal , Fat 7.2g , Sodium 1809mg , Potassium 925mg
Carbohydrates 86 , Protein 8.8g

VEGAN CLAM CHOWDER

15 min	30 min	6

INGREDIENTS

Cream base:
- ½ cup of soaked raw cashews
- ¾ cup of unsweetened soy milk

Mushrooms:
- 1 tablespoon vegan butter
- 1 tablespoon olive oil
- 1 minced garlic clove
- 8 ounces white button mushrooms
- 1 teaspoon low sodium tamari
- 1 teaspoon soy sauce

Soup Base:
- 2 tablespoons vegan butter
- 2 diced celery onions
- 2 medium diced carrots

- 1 medium diced yellow onion
- 3 large, minced cloves garlic
- 1 teaspoon dried thyme
- 3 tablespoons all-purpose flour
- ½ cup dry white wine
- 4 cups low sodium vegetable broth
- 2 medium-sized peeled russet potatoes
- 2 bay leaves
- 2 tablespoons fresh lemon juice
- 2 teaspoons kelp granule or dulse flakes
- 1 teaspoon Himalayan salt
- Fresh cracked pepper

DIRECTIONS

Cream base:
1. Blend the soy milk & cashews until very smooth.
2. Set aside.

Mushrooms:
3. Add 1 tablespoon butter in a large saucepot over medium heat.
4. Add mushrooms when heated and pan-fry until the liquid evaporates.
5. Add 1 clove of minced garlic and soy sauce. Pan fry until the mushrooms are tender & lightly browned.
6. Remove mushrooms and set them aside.

Soup base:
7. Wipe the pot you've used in preparing the mushroom and return to the stove.
8. Heat butter over medium heat.
9. Add onion and pan fry until translucent.
10. Add celery, carrots, garlic & thyme.
11. Pan Fry for about 7 minutes or until veggies are ripe.
12. Add wine

13. Turn heat up to medium-high and leave to simmer.
14. Once it has simmered, turn the heat back to medium.
15. Cook wine down about 5 minutes.
16. Stir it often.
17. Sprinkle flour over veggies
18. Stir constantly for 60 seconds.
19. Stir in broth.
20. Add potatoes, bay leaf, kelp granules, and salt.
21. Bring to a simmer for 15 minutes, until potatoes are tender.
22. Discard bay leaves.
23. Turn heat to medium-low
24. Slowly stir in cashew cream.
25. Taste for seasoning and add more if it is necessary.
26. Cook for 4 minutes.
27. Mix mushrooms, lemon juice, and fresh cracked pepper.
28. Place in your soup bowls & grace with fresh parsley.
29. Side with crackers or crispy bread.

NUTRITION

Calories: 246 , Carbohydrates: 24g , Protein: 9g , Fat: 12g
Sodium: 497mg

VEGAN FISH BURGER WITH HOMEMADE PRETZEL ROLLS

45 min	35 min	

INGREDIENTS

Fish" filets:
- 1 block firm tofu
- ¼ teaspoon dried dill
- 1 teaspoon lemon zest
- ½ cup panko flakes
- ¼ teaspoon salt
- ¼ teaspoon paprika
- 1/3 sheet nori dried seaweed
- ¼ teaspoon mild curry powder
- 2 tablespoons water
- Canola Oil
- 2 tablespoons all-purpose flour

Garlic yogurt sauce:
- 1 teaspoon chopped dill

- 1 minced and roasted garlic clove
- 1/3 cup unsweetened soy yogurt
- Salt

Pretzel rolls:
- 2 ½ cups flour
- 1 teaspoon olive oil
- 2 teaspoons baking soda
- 1 teaspoon pretzel salt
- 1 teaspoon instant yeast
- ½ teaspoon salt
- ¾ lukewarm water
- Lettuce leaves

DIRECTIONS

Pretzel rolls:
1. Mix flour with dry yeast, and salt for the rolls.
2. Add olive oil and 3/4 cup lukewarm water.
3. Mold until a soft dough forms.
4. Leave for about 2 hours until it doubles in size.
5. Preheat the oven to 250 °C.
6. Cut the mold into four equal pieces and form the rolls.
7. Heat the water for the water bath in a small
8. Add in the baking soda.
9. Place the rolls in the hot baking soda water bath, one after the other, with the top side down
10. Let it simmer for about 30 seconds.
11. Place them on a floured baking sheet.
12. Carve the surface of the dough lightly
13. Add the pretzel salt on top.
14. Bake the bread in the oven for about 20 minutes and take it out once the surface is wonderfully golden.

Fish filet:
15. Gently press out excess water from the tofu.
16. Mix the flour with water.
17. Add ½ teaspoon of salt and add more water.
18. Mix the panko flakes, lemon zest, dried dill, curry powder, and paprika powder, salt, and crumbled-up dried seaweed.
19. Cut the tofu into 4 slices and dip them in the egg replacement.
20. Coat them with breadcrumbs.
21. Repeat for all the slices and sauté them in a large pan with olive oil until they're crispy and golden.

Assembling:
22. Mix all the ingredients for the garlic yogurt sauce.
23. Slice the pretzel buns.
24. Add lettuce leaves, followed by the fish filet, and top with the garlic yogurt sauce.

NUTRITION

Calories: 428kcal , Carbohydrates: 74g , Protein: 18g , Fat: 5g
Sodium: 988mg , Potassium: 319mg

CAULIFLOWER CEVICHE

 20 min   5 min   4

INGREDIENTS

- 1 head separated cauliflower
- 1 cup chopped tomatoes
- 1 bunch chopped cilantro
- 1 thinly sliced red onion
- 1 minced jalapeno pepper without seeds
- ½ cup fresh lime juice
- Tortilla chips
- Lime wedges
- Salt

DIRECTIONS

1. Bring a pot with water to a boil
2. Add the cauliflower floret to the boiling water and let cook until they are tender when pierced with a fork
3. Once soft, remove the cauliflower and place in a bowl with ice water to stop the cooking
4. Once they are cool, pat the florets dry with a kitchen towel and chop the cauliflower florets into small pieces.
5. Place the chopped cauliflower, onion, jalapeno, tomatoes, and cilantro and toss together in a large bowl
6. Add the lime juice and salt and toss well to coat and refrigerate until ready to serve
7. Grace with lime wedges and serve with tortilla chips

NUTRITION

Calories: 62kcal , Carbohydrates: 13g , Protein: 3g , Sodium: 47mg
Potassium: 593mg

VEGAN TARTAR SAUCE

 5 min   0 min   6

INGREDIENTS

- 3 small finely chopped pickles
- 1 teaspoon vegan Worcester sauce
- 2 tablespoons freshly squeezed lemon juice
- 1 small finely chopped onion
- 2 teaspoons mustard
- 1 tablespoon pickle juice from the jar
- 1 teaspoon garlic powder
- 1 hand finely chopped dill
- 1 hand finely chopped parsley
- Salt and pepper to taste

Optional additional ingredients for interesting flavors
- 1 teaspoon maple
- 2 teaspoon hot sauce
- 2 tablespoons capers
- 1 tablespoon caper brine

DIRECTIONS

1. Add all ingredients to a bowl.
2. Mix well.

NUTRITION

Calories: 68 , Fat: 7.7g , Carbohydrates: 2.0g

CREAMY FETTUCCINE KING OYSTER MUSHROOM SCALLOPS

🕐 10 min   🍲 20 min   🍽 3

INGREDIENTS

- 8 ounces fettuccine
- 1 ½ cup fresh peas
- 2 tablespoons olive oil
- 2 king oyster mushrooms
- Heavy cashew cream
- 4 minced garlic cloves, minced
- 1 large lemon for juice and zest
- ½ teaspoon red pepper flakes
- 3 ¼ cups low-sodium vege

- table broth
- ¼ cup chopped parsley
- Mineral salt
- Fresh cracked pepper
- ⅓ cup-soaked cashews
- ¼ cup unsweetened Al mond Milk
- ¼ cup Cashew milk
- Juice of ½ small lemon

DIRECTIONS

King Oyster Mushroom Scallops:
1. Gently wash and dry the mush-rooms.
2. Slice into ½ inch pieces.
3. Heat oil over medium heat in pan or pot
4. Add mushrooms and cook until golden.
5. Add 2 tablespoons of water to the pan
6. Repeat as needed when the water has evaporated.
7. Season them with a splash of coconut aminos, low sodium tamari, or pinch of salt.
8. Set the mushrooms aside for now.
Vegan Cream:
9. Put the cashews, almond milk, lemon juice, and some salt in a blender and process until creamy and there are no chunks.
10. Add 1 tbsp. milk a little bit at a time as much as is needed to thin it out to the desired consistency.
11. Set the cream aside.

Pasta:
12. In the same pot, heat the re-maining oil over medium heat
13. Add garlic and red pepper flakes
14. Pan Fry for about 1 minute, or until garlic is golden in color.
15. Add broth and fettuccine and bring to a boil.
16. Cover and reduce heat to a semi-rigorous rolling boil and cook, stirring periodically for about 14 minutes
17. Add the peas and continue to cook.
18. Add the juice of the lemon, heavy cream, mushrooms, salt, to the pan and add fresh cracked pepper to taste.
19. Stir all to combine the flavors and serve.
Serving:
20. Place pasta in individual bowls
21. Top with chopped parsley and a little fresh cracked pepper

NUTRITION

Calories: 434 Kcal , Fat: 10.8 g , Sodium: 152.4 mg
Carbohydrate: 69. 8 g , Protein: 15.5 g

CLEANSING SUSHI ROLL WITH SPICY KALE AND GREEN VEGGIES

🕐 15 min   🍲 0 min   🍽 3

INGREDIENTS

- 1 cup kale packed
- 3 nori sheets
- 1 cucumber
- 1 avocado
- 2 tablespoons vegan mayo
- ½ teaspoon sriracha

DIRECTIONS

1. Prepare the kale salad.
2. Take 1 cup of packed kale and chop finely.
3. Mix kale with 2 tablespoons vegan mayo and 1/2 teaspoon of sriracha in a bowl. Mix until kale is evenly coated.
4. Slice cucumber into thin strips.
5. Slice the avocado into thin chunks as well.
6. Begin to assemble the sushi by spreading out your nori sheets. They need to be oriented so that they are wider than they are tall.
7. Layout the cucumbers, avocado, and kale salad in a strip about 2 inches wide.
8. Place the sushi filling inside the nori with your fingers and tight-ly wrap the nori around the filling with both of your hands.
9. Once the sushi has been sufficiently rolled, slice the sushi, wet-ting your knife between every 2 cuts.
10. Serve sushi with tamari and extra sriracha.

NUTRITION

Calories: 68 Kcal , Fat: 6.7g , Carbohydrates: 1.2g

VEGAN SUSHI BOWL

20 min | 30 min | 1

INGREDIENTS

- 150g or ¾ cup sushi rice
- 200ml scant
- 1 cup water
- 2 tablespoons seasoned vinegar
- ½ (100g) small sweet potato
- A drizzle of vegetable oil
- Rice bran oil
- ¼ cucumber
- 1 carrot
- ½ avocado
- juice of 1 lime
- ½ toasted nori sheet

Extras:
- Tamari sauce
- Wasabi
- Black or white sesame seeds

DIRECTIONS

1. Rinse the rice through a sieve until the water runs clear.
2. Place the rice in a pot with water and warm up over low heat.
3. Cover the pot with a lid and leave for 8 minutes; until the water has been completely absorbed.
4. Set the oven to 150C as the rice is cooking.
5. Peel the sweet potatoes then cut them into disks and halve them.
6. Put the sweet potato pieces into a small bowl.
7. Cover them with some vegetable oil and mix scrupulously.
8. Place them on a baking sheet.
9. Pop them in the oven for 25 minutes; until cooked through and soft.
10. Scrape the rice into a bowl with a wooden spoon.
11. Add the seasoned vinegar and leave to cool to room temperature.
12. Cut the veggies into thin matchsticks or veggie ribbons.
13. Sprinkle the lemon juice over the avocado, half to avoid discoloration and to add some zest.
14. Cover the thin nori strip over the onigiri ball and place it in your bowl.
15. Go through the same procedure until all the rice has been used up.
16. Put together the bowl by adding the veggies and sprinkling them with sesame seeds.
17. Serve with wasabi and tamari sauce.

NUTRITION

Calories: 88.80 Kcal , Carbohydrate: 17.10 g , Fat: 1.39 g Protein: 1.91 g

ROSEMARY & GARLIC MARINATED ALMOND FETA

15 min | 54 min | 4

INGREDIENTS

- Rosemary and Garlic Marinade
- 1 cup almonds (Blanched)
- ¼ cup lemon juice
- 2 large, crushed garlic cloves
- 1 tablespoon olive oil
- 1 teaspoon salt
- 4 tablespoons chopped rosemary leaves
- 1 ½ cups extra virgin olive oil

DIRECTIONS

1. Put the lemon juice, olive oil, almonds, and salt in a high-powered blender.
2. It can be helpful to soak the almonds in water for a few hours before blending so that they are softer.
3. Add ½ cup of water to the previous and blend for about 5 minutes.
4. Place the mixture in a nut milk bag.
5. Squeeze the bag to release the milk.
6. Secure the bag with an elastic band.
7. Place in a colander to drain any excess liquid into the bowl.
8. Refrigerate overnight.
9. On the following day, carefully remove the 'almond feta' from the nut bag and dispose of the drained water.
10. Put the feta in a square-shaped container and compress it so that it takes on the square shape.
11. Put it back in the fridge for 30 minutes to set.
12. Mix the marinade ingredients well.
13. Season to taste with salt and pour into a shallow serving bowl.
14. Cut the large piece of feta into small squares. Be careful, as at this point, it can easily break as it's soft.
15. Cover the squares with the marinade and serve.

NUTRITION

Calories: 170 Kcal , Carbohydrate: 4g , Fat: 17 g , Protein: 3 g

CONCLUSION

CONCLUSION

Plant-based seafood alternatives are nothing new anymore. People have become increasingly interested in sea animal welfare and food sustainability, making it the best big thing on the horizon, becoming a possible remedy for fisherman's exploitation all over the world and an alternative diet to save our seas and oceans.

Already, some innovative minds are taking on this challenge and are offering some plant-based alternatives to popular seafood products, hoping to cut down on the environmental impact of animal production.

REFERENCES

1. https://www.forbes.com/sites/ariellasimke/2020/10/21/everything-you-need-to-know-about-plant-based-seafood/?sh=38ad1d5b7655

2. https://www.animalsaustralia.org/features/plant-based-seafood-recipes.php

3. https://thebeet.com/the-seaspiracy-effect-plant-based-seafood-company-nets-26-million/:~:text=The Seaspiracy Effect%3A Plant-Based Seafood Company Nets %2426 Million&text=The plant-based seafood company,most recent round oht

4. Fehér, A.; Gazdecki, M.; Véha, M.; Szakály, M.; Szakály, Z. A Comprehensive Review of the Benefits of and the Barriers to the Switch to a Plant-Based Diet. Sustainability 2020, 12, 4136.

5. Thavamani, A.; Sferra, T.J.; Sankararaman, S. Meet the Meat Alternatives: The Value of Alternative Protein Sources. Curr. Nutr.Rep. 2020, 9, 346–355.

Made in United States
Troutdale, OR
07/21/2024

21453857R00024